Forensic Entomology: Bugs & Bodies

by Sue Hamilton

Published by ABDO Publishing Company, 8000 West 78th Street, Suite 310, Edina, Minnesota 55439.

Printed in the United States.

Editor: John Hamilton
Series Consultant: Scott Harr, J.D. Criminal Justice Dept Chair, Concordia University St. Paul
Graphic Design: Sue Hamilton
Cover Design: Neil Klinepier
Cover Illustration: iStockphoto
Interior Photos and Illustrations: p 1 Beetles on a bear skull, AP Images; Green bottle fly, iStockphoto; p 3 Beetle, Comstock; p 4 Fly, iStockphoto; p 5 Dr. Jerry Butler, ©2007 University of Florida/IFAS/Thomas Wright; p 6 Maggots in a jar, AP Images; p 7 M. Lee Goff, AP Images; p 8 Fly, iStockphoto; p 9 Chinese farmer, Corbis; p 10 Flea, courtesy Kansas State University; p 11 Plague victim, Photo Researchers, Inc; p 12 Grasshopper, iStockphoto; Termites, Photo Researchers, Inc; p 13 Officer Mel Bishop, AP Images; p 14 Fly feeding, iStockphoto; Locust in soup, iStockphoto; p 15 Grasshopper in hand, iStockphoto; p 16 Dish of maggots, AP Images; p 17 Beekeeper, AP Images; p 18 Ants, iStockphoto; p 19 Crime scene exhibit, AP Images; p 20 Collecting Insects diagram, courtesy Ian Dadour, University of Western Australia; p 21 Maggots on calf liver, ©2007 University of Florida/IFAS/Thomas Wright; p 22 Green bottle fly, iStockphoto; Blowfly laying eggs, Photo Researchers, Inc; p 23 Insect collection, AP Images; p 24 Maggot feeding, Photo Researchers, Inc; p 25 Maggot collection, iStockphoto; p 26 Blowfly emerging from casing, Photo Researchers, Inc; p 27 Blowfly Life Cycle diagram, courtesy The Cleveland Museum of Natural History/Joe Keiper, p 28 Fly, iStockphoto; pp 28-29 Lawyer questioning forensic entomologist M. Lee Goff, AP Images; p 30 Beetle, Comstock; p 32 Beetle, Comstock

Library of Congress Cataloging-in-Publication Data

Hamilton, Sue L., 1959-
  Forensic entomology : bugs & bodies / Sue Hamilton.
    p. cm. -- (Crime scene investigation)
  Includes index.
  ISBN-13: 978-1-59928-991-5
  1. Forensic entomology--Juvenile literature. I. Title.
  RA1063.45.H36 2008
  614'.1--dc22
                        2007035161

CONTENTS

Tattletale Bugs

Bugs don't lie. They don't keep secrets, either. By studying insects, scientists learn many things, including how to help solve crimes. Insects are so predictable and reliable that forensic entomology has become a major part of crime scene investigation.

Entomology is the study of insects. The field of forensics uses science and technology to investigate crimes and provide facts, or evidence, in courtrooms. Combining these two fields of study, the American Board of Forensic Entomology defines its work as "the science of using insect evidence to uncover circumstances of interest to the law, often related to a crime."

Some scientists estimate that Earth holds more than eight million different species of insects. These creatures live everywhere on our planet, but they thrive in warm, moist areas. They are one of the most important parts of Earth's ecosystem. Insects pollinate flowers and aerate the soil. They survive because they have learned to eat almost anything. In fact, one of their most important jobs is to eat—helping rid the world of dead matter. This includes dead plants and animals, including humans.

The behavior of insects is very predictable. When an animal or human dies, especially outdoors when temperatures are warm, it takes as little as 10 minutes before flies begin feeding. Within hours, these flies lay eggs.

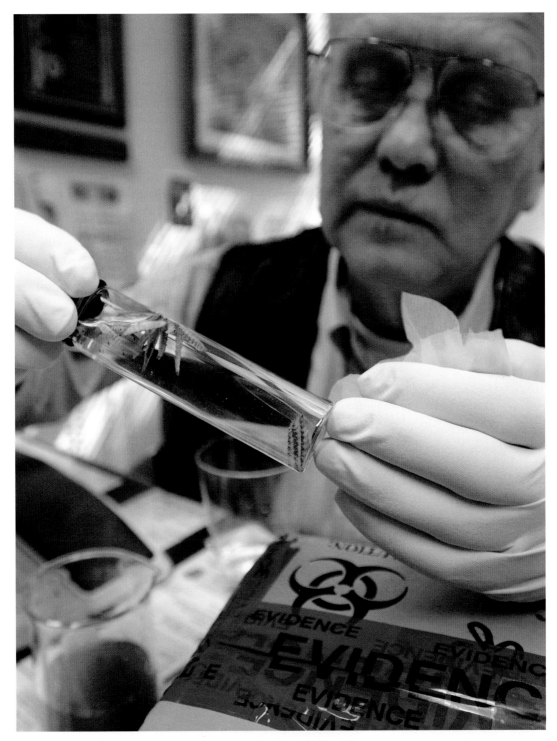

Above: Dr. Jerry Butler from the University of Florida examines hairy maggot blowfly larvae. Butler is one of only five forensic entomologists in Florida.

Below: Maggots, the worm-like stage in a fly's life cycle, crawl around in a jar. To determine age, forensic entomologists sometimes allow specimens to grow to adulthood.

The eggs hatch into first-stage maggots, which feed, grow, and molt into second-stage and third-stage maggots. Finally, the maggots turn into adult flies. The whole process is usually completed in a few days. Forensic entomologists know the flies' life cycle, as well as the life cycles of many other arthropods that have come to feed on the body. These scientists can estimate how much time has passed since a victim died based on what stage of insect life has been found on the corpse.

Not only do insects help provide investigators with a person's estimated time of death, they also give clues about where a crime has been committed, or if a body has been moved. If a bug from another state or region is found on a body, a forensic entomologist might conclude that the body has been moved sometime after the murder. The smallest creatures can sometimes provide the biggest clues for investigators trying to solve crimes.

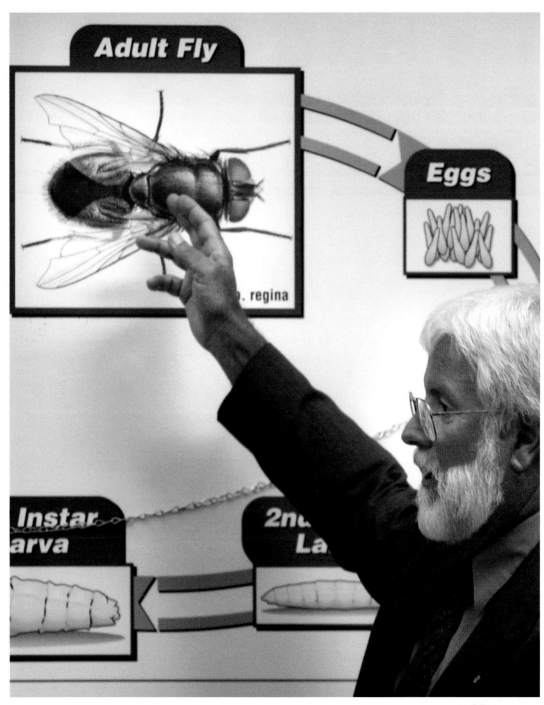

Above: Forensic entomologist M. Lee Goff points to a graphic showing the various stages of a fly's life cycle. Goff estimates how much time has passed since a victim died based on what stage of insect life is found on a dead body.

The History of Forensic Entomology

In the thirteenth century, a Chinese criminologist searched for a murderer in a local village. A body with several deep slashes had been found near a rice field. The investigator questioned a number of people, but had no luck finding the killer. Finally, he brought the villagers together. Each family was instructed to bring their sickles. The investigator believed that the farming tool's sharp, semicircular blade had been the murder weapon. With all the sickles on the ground, the investigator began to look closely at the blades. One sickle attracted a much larger number of flies than the others. Drawn to tiny amounts of the victim's blood and tissue, the flies provided a crucial piece of evidence. The sickle's owner broke down and confessed to the murder.

This case, perhaps the earliest use of forensic entomology, was documented in *The Washing Away of Wrongs,* a book written in 1235 A.D. by criminologist Sung Tz'u. In the same book, Sung also wrote about blowflies and their feeding habits on dead bodies. The book marked the beginning of a field that would become a vital part of crime scene investigation hundreds of years later.

Above: A Chinese farmer stands with a sickle. In the thirteenth century, an investigator found a murderer when insects were attracted to blood on the farmer's sickle.

Above: A flea. These tiny blood-sucking insects, transported on the backs of rats, were carriers of the bubonic plague, or Black Death. Over the years, the plague caused the deaths of millions of people.

Throughout recorded history, several major outbreaks of disease have killed huge numbers of people. From about 1347 to 1353 A.D., bubonic plague, also known as the Black Death, spread across Europe, central Asia, and the Middle East, wiping out millions of people. In Europe alone, an estimated 20 million people died from this nearly unstoppable epidemic.

Over the centuries, the Black Death returned several times to wreak even more misery. London, England, was a city of disease and death from 1592 to 1594, and again from 1664 to 1665. Sights of the dead were commonplace. Many people fell dead in the streets and fields, their bodies left to rot by fearful survivors. Insects lived off the decaying corpses. Doctors, law enforcement officials, artists, and authors studied, wrote about, and illustrated the effects of bugs on the dead.

In more modern times, one of the first uses of forensic entomology was in France, in 1850. Dr. Marcel Bergeret, a medical doctor and naturalist with an interest in insects, was called to an apartment where a repairman had uncovered the remains of a newborn baby left behind a fireplace mantel. Four different couples had lived in the apartment over a period of three years, but the horrified man and woman currently residing there were suddenly murder suspects.

Dry, warm air circulating through the chimney had mummified the baby's body. At first, neither the local medical examiner nor Dr. Bergeret could provide a time of death. Then Dr. Bergeret had an idea: he studied insects and their eggs collected from the corpse. Based on this evidence, he estimated that two generations of insects must have lived on the remains.

Left: An illustration of the misery the Black Death brought in 1349. A father carries a plague-ridden child down a street where a woman lies dead. Fearfully, a man steps aside and covers his face.

Bergeret concluded that the body had been behind the wall for two years, which proved the innocence of the current apartment dwellers. An arrest warrant was issued for the people who had lived there two years earlier.

Throughout the nineteenth and twentieth centuries, studies of insect life on dead bodies continued. Today, forensic entomologists regularly use their knowledge of insect life cycles to assist in crime scene investigations.

A Science for Bug Lovers

Forensic entomologists are a rare group. A worldwide directory lists less than 70 scientists actively involved in this field. Most of these professionals also work as college teachers and researchers. Law enforcement agencies usually employ forensic entomologists as needed, on a case-by-case basis. These insect specialists work in three different areas: urban, stored-product, and medicolegal/medicocriminal.

Urban: City Pests

Entomologists who specialize in urban forensics work in cities. They are insect specialists who work on court cases involving bug problems with people's homes and workplaces. For example, an infestation of cockroaches, fleas, or other arthropods in an apartment is a health problem. If a landlord has been asked to correct the situation and does nothing, a renter has the right to sue the landlord. Another example may be when a homeowner brings charges against a pest-control service that was paid to take care of a termite infestation, but did not rid the house of the bugs. To termites, a house is like a giant all-you-can-eat buffet. They love wood, paper, and carpeting. Serious and costly damage can occur. A forensic entomologist may be asked to appear in court to help explain what damages were caused by the insects, and exactly when the damages occurred.

Below: Termites feast on wood. Forensic entomologists may be called into court to report damage made by these insects on people's homes.

Above: Officer Mel Bishop of Charlottesville, Virginia, holds up a jar of maggots. Bishop, an entomologist, uses the insects to help determine a victim's time of death.

Stored-Product: Pests in the Package

A forensic entomologist may specialize in inspecting foods that are sold in restaurants and grocery stores. The food may be infested or contaminated with insects, their eggs, or larvae. There are countless insects in the air, ground, and foods that we harvest. It is almost impossible to manufacture food products without some trace of insects in the package. In the United States, the Food and Drug Administration (FDA) strictly regulates how many animal and insect parts can be in foods. Foods that are highly contaminated may result in criminal or civil court cases. For example, if a person opens a can of soup and finds a dead fly mixed in with the vegetables and broth, the disgusted customer may file charges against the manufacturer. However, the manufacturer may claim that the consumer put the fly in the soup at home. A forensic entomologist may be called to try to find out where the insect entered the soup.

Below: A bowl of soup with a locust floating in it. In stored-product cases, forensic entomologists may be asked to help determine where bugs entered the food in question.

Medicolegal/Medicocriminal: Bugs and Murder

This area combines medicine, law, and criminal activity. It is probably the most well-known part of a forensic entomologist's job. Insect evidence is collected, preserved, and analyzed from bodies and crime scenes. The insect specialist studies the bugs and works with criminal investigators, medical examiners, and coroners to estimate when, and sometimes where, a person died. Forensic entomologists may also link a victim and a suspect based on insect remains. For example, while collecting evidence from a murder victim in Texas, the crushed remains of a grasshopper were found in the folds of the woman's clothing. The grasshopper's body parts were collected. At first, this did not seem to be an important piece of evidence. In the course of the investigation, the police questioned several suspects. During a routine search of one suspect, a grasshopper's left hind leg was recovered from the cuff of the person's pants. Coincidentally, this was the only part missing from the grasshopper collected off the victim. A close check showed that the break mark between the grasshopper's body and leg matched exactly, proving that the suspect had been present during the woman's murder. The suspect was arrested, tried, and convicted of murder.

Above: A green grasshopper. Finding an insect unique to a certain area at a crime scene may help forensic entomologists determine that a body has been moved.

Below: A researcher holds a dish of maggots. Forensic entomologists may find traces of drugs from maggots collected off crime scene victims.

This area of forensic entomology may also include the use of insects to understand what happened under unusual circumstances. For example, in the winter of 1990, the body of a young man was found in a wooded area in Connecticut. There were no signs of foul play—no knife or bullet wounds. How did he die? Maggots feeding off the body provided a clue. Traces of cocaine were found in the insects. A background check revealed that the man had used drugs in the past. His death was ruled an accidental overdose.

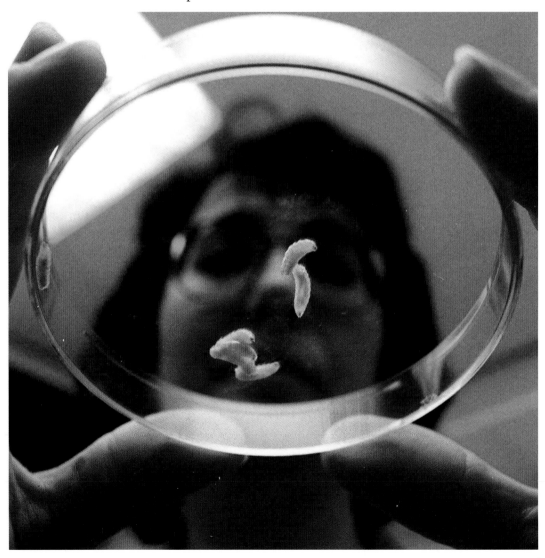

Sometimes insects *create* crime scenes. Serious, even deadly, traffic accidents are occasionally reported where drivers lose control of their vehicles for no clear reason. At first, investigators suspect that the drivers or the vehicles are at fault. Did the drivers fall asleep at the wheel? Were they drinking and driving? Did the brakes fail? Any of these reasons may be possible, but if bees, or parts of bee bodies, are found in the car, investigators know the responsibility may lie with the tiny insects. Bees fly in open car windows, frightening everyone inside. It's easy to see how an accident can happen when an angry bee buzzes frantically in a car, terrifying or stinging the driver or passengers. One driver even had a bee fly in his car window, land on his cheek, and then crawl under his sunglasses. Only supreme self-control kept the driver from having an accident.

Above: A beekeeper begins the process of taking a swarm of bees off a parked car in downtown San Francisco, California. The area was roped off by police until the bees could be removed.

Insects and Postmortem Interval

The amount of time that has passed since a person has died is called the postmortem interval (PMI). This knowledge is critical in murder investigations. Knowing when a death occurred helps law enforcement officers center their investigation on suspects who cannot confirm their whereabouts at the time of the murder. A suspect may have an alibi for one period of time, but not hours earlier or later. Crime scene investigators have several ways to determine the time of death.

If a body is found within 24 hours of death, a core temperature reading is taken. Typically, a body cools slowly after death. Factoring in the surrounding area's temperature and the size of the body, forensic scientists can usually estimate the time of death based on this temperature reading.

Rigor mortis, the slow stiffening of a corpse's muscles, may also provide time of death. For the first three hours after death, the muscles stay relaxed. In the next 3 to 36 hours, they stiffen because of a chemical change inside the muscle tissue. After about 36 hours, the muscles begin to relax again. However, the onset of *rigor mortis* varies depending on the condition of the muscles prior to death.

Facing Page:
A forensic entomology exhibit in Chicago, Illinois. The exhibit recreated an actual crime scene where visitors could learn how investigators use the presence of insects in different stages of life to help determine the circumstances of death.

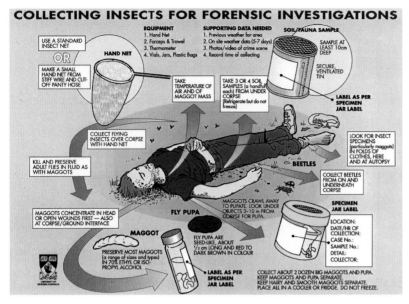

Above: A diagram showing the steps taken to collect insects for forensic investigations.

Insect life on a dead body offers yet another way to estimate the PMI. Detailed studies give clues to investigators about the kind of insect life to expect on corpses within certain time periods. However, insect activity varies depending on the weather and a body's location. A corpse lying in the sun on a hot, humid day will host insect activity within a few minutes. On the other hand, a plastic-wrapped body buried in a snowbank in the dead of winter will have little insect activity.

Crime scene investigators collect a great deal of information on the bugs found at a death scene. This includes insect activity in, on, and under the corpse, as well as insect activity within 10 to 20 feet (3 to 6 m) of the body. Collections are made of insects that are resting or crawling in the area. Investigators use insect nets to sweep the air and collect samples of insects flying near the body.

If present, maggots of various sizes are collected. Some are preserved in specimen jars filled with alcohol. Others are kept alive. Since flies go through several stages before reaching adulthood, it is sometimes difficult to know how many hours or days old they are when they are still in their worm-like maggot form. Forensic entomologists allow a number of the biggest, and thus oldest, maggots to grow to adulthood in the lab. By tracking the amount of time that passes from

the maggot stage to the adult fly stage, scientists are able to estimate how long flies have been on a body before the maggots were collected.

Insects are often collected by a medical examiner during an autopsy. Sometimes this yields surprises. Bugs find their way into a body through any opening—natural (eyes, ears, nose, mouth, and genitals) and unnatural (cuts or bullet wounds). Small breaks in the skin may go unnoticed by investigators, but the presence of bugs often leads to further examinations. Forensic scientists may find clues about the types of murder weapons used or entry points for poison.

Above: A researcher from the University of Florida checks a colony of blowfly maggots feeding on calf liver. The entomologist is studying the maggots' growth rates at various temperatures.

Blowflies

A blowfly can pick up the faintest odor of animal or human decay from a distance of more than one mile (1.6 km). Female blowflies need to find freshly dead, still-moist corpses in which to lay their eggs. Because flies, especially blowflies, are often the first insects to find dead bodies, a great deal of forensic study has been conducted on their predictable life cycle. Blowflies give very accurate clues about the time that has passed since an animal or human has died.

Here is what a forensic entomologist may expect to find on a dead body lying outside on a warm, humid summer day:

Below: A colored scanning electron micrograph (SEM) of a female blowfly laying her eggs (lower left.)

0 to 60 Minutes: Blowflies Discover the Body

Adult blowflies move in, frantically feeding on any proteins, such as blood, sweat, and tears, oozing from the body.

10 to 60 Minutes: Eggs are Laid

Female blowflies lay tiny mounds of 200 to 500 eggs in natural openings on the body, as well as in any open wounds. The white-to-yellowish egg clumps look like small rice balls. Each of the tiny eggs is no longer than 2 millimeters (.08 inches).

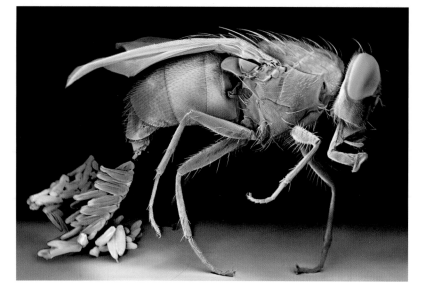

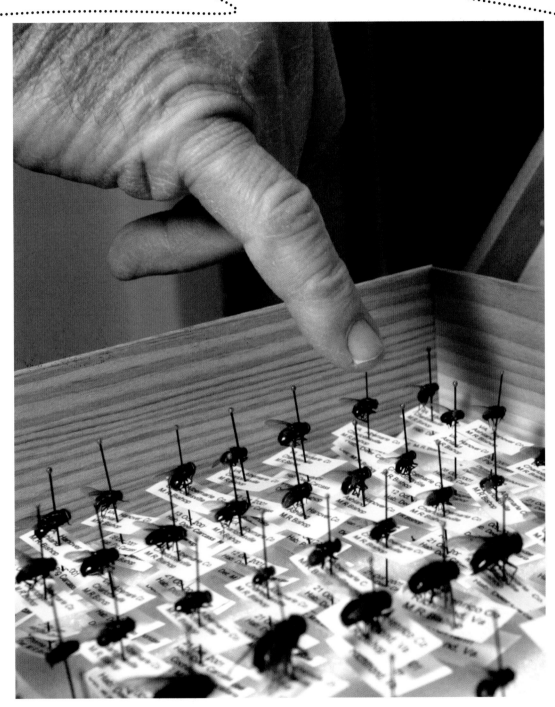

Above: Charlottesville, Virginia, city police officer Mel Bishop points to pinned insect samples used to identify and match bugs found on dead bodies. Bishop is an expert in the science of entomology and uses bugs found on dead bodies to determine how long a person has been dead.

Right: Colored scanning electron micrograph (SEM) of a Calliphora vicina blowfly maggot (larva) feeding on liver tissue. A blowfly lays its eggs on dead bodies, and this behavior is studied by forensic entomologists. A blowfly maggot can grow quickly, developing from egg to pupa in two to three weeks. The growth rate depends on the type of fly and the surrounding temperature. The size of a maggot and the temperature allows forensic entomologists to estimate the host body's time of death.

One Day: First Instar Stage

During this first stage of development, the blowfly eggs hatch into maggots. These 5 mm- (.2 inch-) long, worm-like larvae immediately begin feeding on the corpse. A maggot's outside layer is called the cuticle. Cuticles are made of chitin, a flexible substance that protects the maggots from the environment. It does not grow the way human skin does. As the larvae feed on dead tissues, they quickly outgrow and shed their cuticles. This is known as molting. The larger maggots now have larger cuticles to grow into. Typically after one day, forensic investigators see the first molted casings of the small but growing larvae.

Two to Three Days:
Second Instar Stage
Maggots continue to feed, doubling in size to approximately 10 mm (.4 inches) in length. At the end of this stage, they molt once again.

Four to Five Days: Third Instar Stage
Maggots feed and grow to their biggest size: 17 mm (.67 inch). The mass of large bugs often creates heat, raising the temperature of the surrounding tissue. Temperature on the body can increase up to an additional 50 degrees Fahrenheit (10 degrees C).

Above: A collection of maggots. From the first instar stage to the third instar stage, maggots will more than triple in size.

Below: A colored scanning electron micrograph (SEM) of a blowfly beginning to emerge from the top of its pupal case.

8 to 12 Days: Prepupa Stage

Also known as the post-feeding, or wandering, stage, this is when the maggots stop feeding and shrink in size to about 12 mm (.47 inches). They leave the corpse, which is now attracting other predators who might feast on the larvae. The maggots seek a safe, dry area to finish their transformation into an adult. Investigators may find them on the ground, on rocks, or in surrounding trees or vegetation.

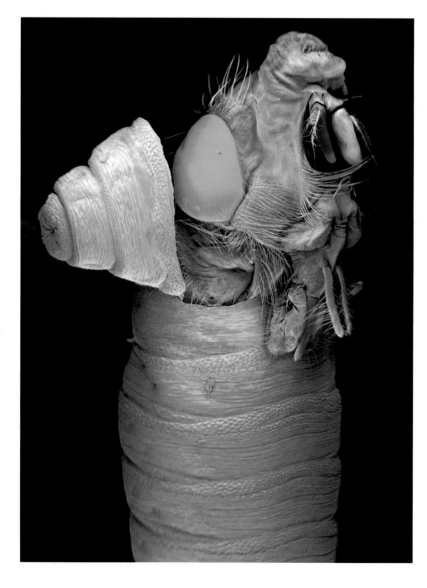

18 to 24 Days: Pupa Stage

After finding an acceptable place safely away from the decomposing corpse, the maggots begin to form pupae. This is the insect form between larva and adult. Each pupa is about 9 mm (.35 inches) in length. The outside shells harden and slowly turn from their original white or light-yellow color to a darker reddish-brown color.

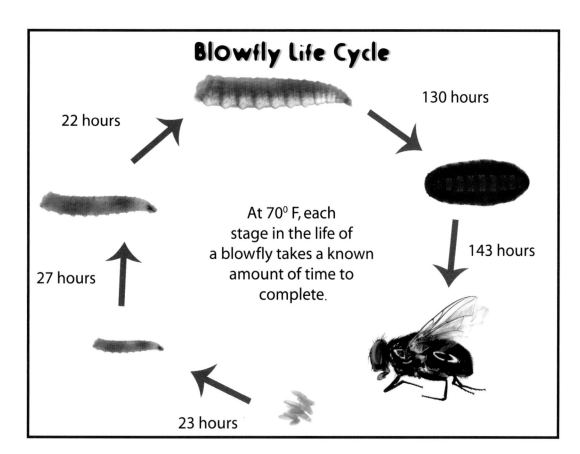

Blowfly Life Cycle

22 hours

130 hours

At 70° F, each stage in the life of a blowfly takes a known amount of time to complete.

143 hours

27 hours

23 hours

This pupal case color provides a timing clue to forensic entomologists. The more time that passes, the darker the color.

Adult

At the end of the pupa stage, the maggot shape is gone. The larvae have undergone metamorphosis, emerging from the casings as adult flies. However, they do not yet look like true adults.

At first, a blowfly's body is soft, its cuticle is lightly colored, and its wings are wrinkled and collapsed. The blowfly needs this soft flexibility in order to escape the hard pupa casing. In the next several hours, the wings smooth out and expand, the cuticle hardens, and the fly becomes an adult that is able to take wing. In 5 to 18 days, this adult fly begins reproducing. The female fly will seek another dead body on which to lay her eggs, and begin the entire cycle again.

Above: Typical blowfly life cycle. Growth rate for flies is dependent on temperature. To estimate the PMI, an investigator must know the temperature around the body for the time period in question.

Bugs On a Body

Skilled forensic entomologists know that, in general, over the course of several days insects such as flies, beetles, mites, wasps, and moths descend on exposed dead bodies. However, an entomologist's job is not as simple as identifying the bugs on a body and estimating how long they have been there. Scientists note that many different factors may change the timing of these stages.

Fly eggs may begin to develop on a body one day, but then suddenly the weather turns cooler. The eggs may stop growing for a few hours, or even days, until the weather warms up, and then continue their life cycle pattern. By focusing only on the maggots' development, it may appear that the body has been dead for a day or two, when in fact it may have been several days.

Forensic entomologists also pay attention to the fact that a body may be more decomposed than the insect life shows it

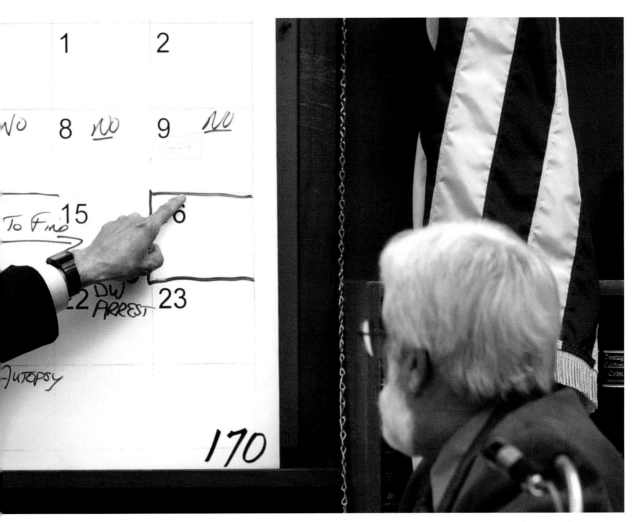

should be. This could mean that the body was stored for some time and then placed outside. If all the information doesn't add up, some part of the puzzle is still missing.

In his book, *A Fly for the Prosecution,* forensic entomologist M. Lee Goff states, "…what I produce is an estimate not of the postmortem interval, but of the time insects have been active on the corpse. Frequently the two are very close, but sometimes the period of insect activity is significantly different from the postmortem interval." Forensic entomologists provide one important part of a case, but it takes a complete crime scene investigation to find all the answers.

Above: A lawyer questions forensic entomologist M. Lee Goff in court regarding the insects he found on a murder victim.

GLOSSARY

AERATE — To add air into a material, such as the ground.

ALIBI — Proof that a person was somewhere else when a criminal act took place.

ARTHROPODS — A group of animals that includes insects, spiders, and crustaceans. Arthropods have an external skeleton, a segmented body, and jointed limbs.

AUTOPSY — An exam performed on a dead body to find out the cause of death.

BLACK DEATH — An outbreak of bubonic plague. The deadly disease, spread mainly by fleas on rats, killed millions of people in the fourteenth to early nineteenth centuries. Victims suffered from fever, stomach cramps, and boils, but it was the dark patches covering their bodies that brought about the name "Black Death."

CIVIL LAWSUIT — A noncriminal lawsuit that usually involves issues between members of a community, often concerning property rights.

CORPSE — A dead body.

CRIMINOLOGIST — A person who studies crimes and criminals to understand how these people think and behave. A criminologist's work helps law enforcement find and capture criminals by predicting what they may do in certain situations.

DECOMPOSE — A process that happens after death when a body begins to rot, breaking down into its most basic elements.

ECOSYSTEM — An area of living plants, animals, and other organisms that interact with each other and their non-living environment.

EVIDENCE — Objects, and sometimes information, that helps prove the details and facts in a legal investigation.

INFEST — Large numbers of bugs or other unwanted animals that invade places or products where they create an unhealthy situation.

INSTAR — A stage of insect development. Each instar ends with the molt or shedding of the insect's old skin. Different insects have different numbers of instars. Blowflies have three instar stages. Beetles typically have 3 to 5 instars, but some beetles have as many as 30 instars.

LARVAE — The worm-like form of many insects when they are newly hatched, prior to the bugs changing into their winged, adult shape.

LAWSUIT — A legal way to settle a dispute in which both sides argue their case in front of a judge or jury in a court of law. The person who has been wronged is called the plaintiff. The person being sued is called the defendant. Plaintiffs and defendants can be individuals, or they can be businesses or government entities, such as corporations or towns.

MAGGOT — The soft-bodied, legless larva of a blowfly or housefly, usually found in decaying tissue.

MEDICAL EXAMINER — A medical doctor authorized to find the cause of death of bodies whose deaths are not related to natural causes.

METAMORPHOSIS — The process an insect goes through to change from how it looks when it hatches out of the egg to its final adult shape.

MUMMIFIED — A process where most of the water has been removed from an animal or human body. Mummification retains the body's shape and preserves it for a long period of time.

PLAGUE — A serious, often deadly, disease that is easily passed from person to person.

PREDICTABLE — To behave in a way that is expected.

SUE — To bring a lawsuit against a person or institution in a court of law.

INDEX